SECRETS
OF THE
ANIMAL WORLD

STORKS
Majestic Migrators

by Eulalia García
Illustrated by Gabriel Casadevall and Ali Garousi

Gareth Stevens Publishing
MILWAUKEE

For a free color catalog describing Gareth Stevens' list of high-quality books and multimedia programs, call 1-800-542-2595 (USA) or 1-800-461-9120 (Canada). Gareth Stevens Publishing's Fax: (414) 225-0377. See our catalog, too, on the World Wide Web: http://gsinc.com

The editor would like to extend special thanks to Jan W. Rafert, Curator of Primates and Small Mammals, Milwaukee County Zoo, Milwaukee, Wisconsin, for his kind and professional help with the information in this book.

Library of Congress Cataloging-in-Publication Data

García, Eulalia.
    [Cigüeña]. English]
    Storks: majestic migrators / by Eulalia García; illustrated by Gabriel Casadevall and Ali Garousi.
        p. cm. – (Secrets of the animal world)
    Includes bibliographical references and index.
    Summary: Provides information on the physical characteristics and behavior of storks, focusing on their annual migrations.
    ISBN 0-8368-1587-4 (lib. bdg.)
    1. Storks–Juvenile literature. 2. Birds–Migration–Juvenile literature. [1. Storks. 2. Birds–Migration.] I. Casadevall, Gabriel, ill. II. Garousi, Ali, ill. III. Title. IV. Series.
QL696.C535G3713 1996
598.3'4–dc20   96-8198

This North American edition first published in 1996 by
Gareth Stevens Publishing
1555 North RiverCenter Drive, Suite 201
Milwaukee, Wisconsin 53212 USA

This U.S. edition © 1996 by Gareth Stevens, Inc. Created with original © 1993 Ediciones Este, S.A., Barcelona, Spain. Additional end matter © 1996 by Gareth Stevens, Inc.

Series editor: Patricia Lantier-Sampon
Editorial assistants: Diane Laska, Rita Reitci

Printed in the United States of America

1 2 3 4 5 6 7 8 9 99 98 97 96

CONTENTS

BIRDS AND MIGRATION

Where do birds migrate?

Migrating birds travel hundreds or even thousands of miles (kilometers) each year from their nesting grounds to their winter quarters. They return in spring to the nesting grounds. For example, the golden plover travels from the Arctic all the way to South America — 5,600 miles (9,000 km) away.

In Europe, the common stork heads for Africa in the autumn, crossing the Mediterranean Sea

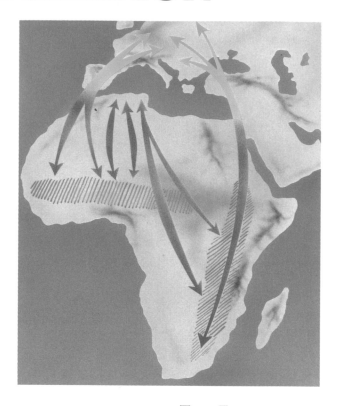

Two European stork populations reach Africa by different routes, flying over land as much as possible.

Gulls, such as this Sabine's gull, also migrate. They leave polar regions to spend winter in the tropics.

Although the eider duck can fly, it swims over long distances during migration.

Storks can travel long distances easily. Their large, wide wings allow them to glide without wasting energy.

at its narrowest point. Another stork species reaches Africa by traveling along the Strait of Bosporus and the Nile River.

The Northern Hemisphere has a greater land area, so there are more birds to migrate. The birds travel from the north toward the equator. Migration in the Southern Hemisphere is the opposite of that in the north; animals travel from the south toward the equator. Birds usually fly when they migrate, but some, such as penguins, swim. Migrations by foot are not usual, although one type of American coot actually walks to its winter home.

Some migratory birds

When autumn arrives in the Northern Hemisphere, many birds begin a long journey to warmer lands to avoid the cold winter. Estival birds remain in one place only for the summer. Sedentary birds remain in the same place all year. Winter birds move from the far North to spend warmer winters elsewhere in the Northern Hemisphere.

Storks travel more than 6,215 miles (10,000 km) from their nesting grounds in Europe to Africa for the winter. Bee-eater hawks migrate in large

Some migratory birds travel long distances and cross the equator. Others stay in the Northern Hemisphere.

COMMON SWALLOW

COMMON STORK

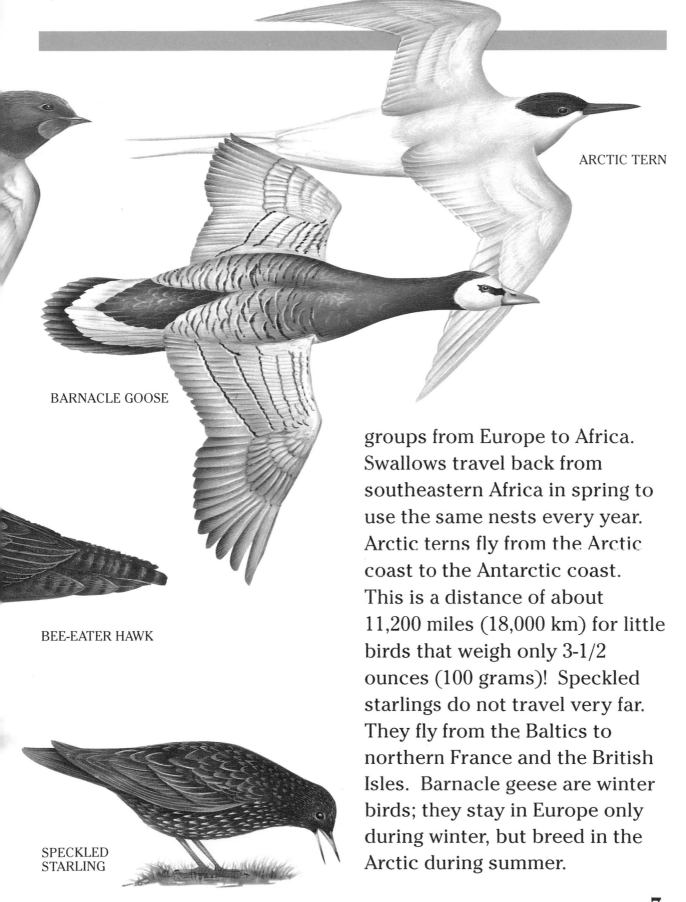

ARCTIC TERN

BARNACLE GOOSE

BEE-EATER HAWK

SPECKLED STARLING

groups from Europe to Africa. Swallows travel back from southeastern Africa in spring to use the same nests every year. Arctic terns fly from the Arctic coast to the Antarctic coast. This is a distance of about 11,200 miles (18,000 km) for little birds that weigh only 3-1/2 ounces (100 grams)! Speckled starlings do not travel very far. They fly from the Baltics to northern France and the British Isles. Barnacle geese are winter birds; they stay in Europe only during winter, but breed in the Arctic during summer.

INSIDE THE STORK

Storks are majestic migratory birds that live near well-watered, cultivated land. Their migratory patterns are well known. Birds and other living creatures have a type of internal "alarm clock" that decides certain activities. This "clock" tells the birds when it is time to migrate. Birds always follow the correct path, even if it is their first migration and they are alone.

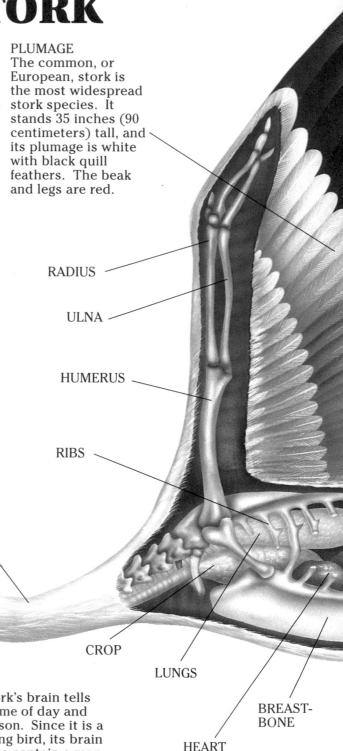

PLUMAGE
The common, or European, stork is the most widespread stork species. It stands 35 inches (90 centimeters) tall, and its plumage is white with black quill feathers. The beak and legs are red.

RADIUS

ULNA

HUMERUS

RIBS

NECK

EYES
The stork has good eyesight, like most birds. As a migratory bird, the stork may also have a special organ on the retina to help it determine the sun's position.

CROP

LUNGS

BREAST-BONE

HEART

BEAK
Beak is long, straight, and heavy. The stork uses it to capture prey. Males and females clack their beaks when they greet each other in the nest.

BRAIN
The stork's brain tells it the time of day and the season. Since it is a migrating bird, its brain may also contain a map of the sky to guide it during migration.

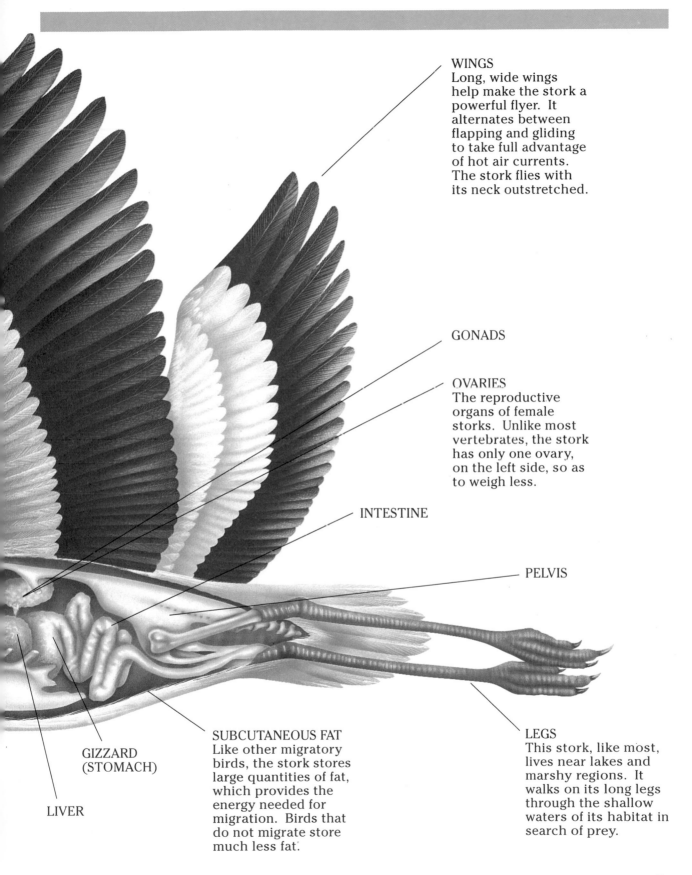

WINGS
Long, wide wings
help make the stork a
powerful flyer. It
alternates between
flapping and gliding
to take full advantage
of hot air currents.
The stork flies with
its neck outstretched.

GONADS

OVARIES
The reproductive
organs of female
storks. Unlike most
vertebrates, the stork
has only one ovary,
on the left side, so as
to weigh less.

INTESTINE

PELVIS

LEGS
This stork, like most,
lives near lakes and
marshy regions. It
walks on its long legs
through the shallow
waters of its habitat in
search of prey.

SUBCUTANEOUS FAT
Like other migratory
birds, the stork stores
large quantities of fat,
which provides the
energy needed for
migration. Birds that
do not migrate store
much less fat.

**GIZZARD
(STOMACH)**

LIVER

ROUTES AND ORIENTATION

How do migrating birds find their way?

Both experienced adult birds and young ones traveling for the first time are driven by the same need to move from one place to another, or migrate. Their main reason is a lack of food, such as insects and seeds, because of the changing seasons. Except for birds that are unable to fly and those living in tropical forests, about four thousand of

Some small birds migrate in stages, stopping to eat and drink before crossing dry areas.

the eight thousand existing bird species migrate.

Scientists have discovered that birds guide themselves

Insects become scarce in winter, so many birds, like this bee-eater, migrate to warmer areas.

during migration by the position of the sun during the day and by the moon and stars at night. Some believe birds use Earth's magnetic field, but this has not been proven. The length of daytime affects the birds' decision to start the journey. Changes in the amount of daylight time produce hormonal changes in the bird, which then feels the need to migrate.

Birds find their bearings by observing the position of the moon and stars by night and the sun's position by day.

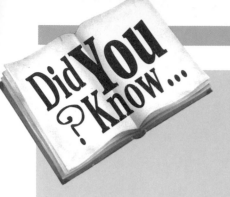

that there
are bald storks?

Marabou and storks belong to the same family, but they do not look like relatives. The marabou's head and neck are pale pink with no feathers. The lack of feathers on the marabou's head may be to prevent it from getting covered with blood when it puts its head inside a carcass to eat. Marabou can be seen prowling around African villages for garbage and in recently burned-over areas for animal remains to eat.

Home again

Birds traveling toward their nesting grounds in spring usually travel faster than when they are heading toward their winter quarters. They are eager to find their nests. From an early age, birds memorize details of their nest's surroundings so they can find the same place year after year.

Some birds, such as starlings, fly in large flocks to protect themselves from enemies, but other birds fly alone or in couples. Storks fly in flocks.

Many large birds fly alone, but these cranes migrate in groups and stay together to find a feeding place after the hard journey.

The males and females of some bird species, but not all, migrate together.

Migratory birds have a good memory and can recognize the exact place where they nested the previous year.

HOW BIRDS MIGRATE

Departure times

Migratory birds starting their journey need calm weather and a wind blowing in the right direction. An overcast sky, rain, or fog can make the birds turn around and fly back to their starting point.

Some birds fly in a V-formation, others in lines, and some, like the swallows, in large flocks that cloud the sky.

The drive to migrate varies with age and the time of year. Adults set off earlier than young birds. Storks leave in broad daylight to make use of warm air currents not found at night.

Nighttime migrators include flycatchers, swallows, and whitethroats, which usually travel for only a few hours at a time. Swifts cover about 60 miles (96 km) a day, and others

cover 185 to 370 miles (300 to 600 km) daily, stopping to eat and rest.

Some birds form a line when traveling long distances. Many ducks fly in a slanting line; swans and geese in a V-shaped line. Birds in front change places every so often with others in the same flight. Many young birds migrate alone, such as the cuckoos. In the stork and some other species, fledglings and adults migrate together.

This young cuckoo will migrate from Europe to South Africa alone.

that storks return to the same nests every year?

In spring, storks arrive in the same places they nested in the previous year. They even look for the same nests they used before. Storks build their nests in eight days in trees, roofs, or bell towers. If occupying an old nest, they use twigs to repair and enlarge it. Some of these nests weigh over 1,000 pounds (450 kg). The males are the first to arrive at the nest, clacking their beaks while waiting for the females to arrive.

Speed and altitude

To avoid obstacles, birds that migrate at night usually fly at a higher altitude than those flying by day. To go faster when returning to their nesting grounds, they also fly higher than when heading for their winter quarters.

Small birds generally fly below 330 feet (100 m); larger birds, such as birds of prey, can be seen at altitudes of 2,625 feet (800 m). Storks usually fly at about 3,280 feet (1,000 m), and cranes have been seen at a height of 13,125 feet (4,000 m) above sea level.

Small birds with short wings fly low. Large birds, however, can reach great heights when gliding.

Although small, swifts fly at great altitudes. When migrating, they make use of air currents and can fly at 3,935 feet (1,200 m).

THE FIRST MIGRATIONS

Evolution of migration

Why did birds begin migrating? Migration uses up a lot of energy and exposes the birds to danger from predators during the long journey. But migration also has an advantage: when food becomes scarce at a certain time of year, migrating birds can fly to areas with plentiful food sources. This gives them a better chance for survival.

There are two main theories about the origins of migration. According to one theory, birds first lived in the Northern Hemisphere. When the land iced over, they moved south. When the ice melted, they returned to

In spite of the dangers of migration, birds leave their breeding grounds in autumn to spend winter in the south. They return in spring to nest.

There are two theories about the origins of migration: 1) birds lived in the Northern Hemisphere and migrated south; 2) the birds' habitat was in the tropics, and they moved north in search of food. Today, neither theory is totally accepted.

the north. Another theory says that birds lived in the tropics, but became so numerous that they had to go north to search for food.

Migratory birds do not always occupy the same area. Young birds tend to travel farther than adults. They can lose their way and so colonize remote areas.

that there are black storks?

Unlike the common, or European, stork, which is white except for the wings, black storks have only a white breast and tail. Neck feathers are bright metallic colors, and a red mask wraps around the eyes to the beak. Black storks live in remote places, nesting on cliffs and treetops, close to fresh water. Their nests are made of branches and earth, with a bedding of soft moss.

STORK BEHAVIOR

Hello, I'm here!

The stork's dramatic, sometimes flashy, behavior can attract a lot of attention — from humans as well as other storks. One gesture is flinging back its head and noisily clacking its beak in greeting. This happens when one of a pair of storks returns to the nest after a long absence, usually when searching for food. It is a friendly gesture.

Storks capture prey in lagoons and marshes, sometimes far from their nests and nesting grounds.

When storks greet one another, they clack their beaks together, making a rattling sound for several seconds.

The grasshopper bird

Stork couples meet again in spring in the same place as the previous year. When they arrive, they greet one another with a clacking of beaks to begin the mating ceremony. After mating, the female lays between six and eight eggs, which hatch after thirty days. Both parents incubate the eggs and feed the chicks. During this time, the stork's diet ranges from aquatic vertebrates to earthworms. In its winter home, however, it chases locusts. This is how the stork earns its nickname of "grasshopper bird."

While one parent looks for food, the other guards the young against any outside danger.

These stork chicks wait to be fed by their parents. They will soon be ready for their first annual migration to Africa.

Other storks

There are seventeen different species of storks living in all parts of the world except in the coldest regions. The male and female African jabiru, or saddlebill storks, are exactly alike except for one feature: the males have dark eyes, and the females have yellow. The saddlebill eats fish that it swallows head first, always followed by a drink of water. The openbill stork has a bill that does not close all the way. It can open freshwater snails and mussels that it finds by raking around in the mud.

The openbill stork's beak is as sharp as a knife. This helps it cut through the tough shells of its aquatic prey.

This saddlebill stork searches for food in shallow waters.

APPENDIX TO

SECRETS OF THE ANIMAL WORLD

ANIMAL WORLD

STORKS
Majestic Migrators

BIRD SECRETS

Making friends. Some ducks may change their nesting grounds when they mate with females from another group. These ducks will leave to breed at the females' nesting grounds instead of their own.

▼ **The crest of the hoopoe**. This migratory bird has a crest of feathers that it unfolds when fighting with males over territory and when courting females, offering them food.

▼ **Birds with ID cards**. Ornithologists put rings on a bird's leg to record the place and date of capture. This way, they can track its route, how long it takes, and its destination.

▼ **Rest instead of migration.** Not all birds migrate for the winter. The nightjar, for example, falls into a deep sleep instead.

Little migrators. Not all migratory birds are as large as the storks. The ruby-ruffed hummingbird, only 3 inches (7.5 cm) long, nests in the south of Canada and spends the winter 1,550 miles (2,500 km) away in Florida.

▶ **Look out, the sparrow hawk is coming!** Starlings travel in widespread flocks. However, when their powerful enemy, the sparrow hawk, approaches, they group together so that they cannot be attacked.

1. Migrating birds guide themselves by:
a) the sun.
b) the moon and stars.
c) the sun, moon, and stars.

2. In autumn, the common stork heads for:
a) Africa.
b) South America.
c) the British Isles.

3. Migratory birds travel fastest:
a) when they are going to their winter quarters.
b) when they are heading for the nesting grounds.
c) when they are searching for food.

4. Birds migrate because:
a) food is scarce.
b) they don't like to be crowded.
c) they are hot.

5. When common storks greet one another, they do so:
a) without making any noise.
b) by clacking their beaks and flinging back their heads.
c) by jumping up and down in their nests.

6. Which birds migrate at night?
a) Storks.
b) Flycatchers, swallows, and whitethroats.
c) No bird travels at night.

The answers to BIRD SECRETS questions are on page 32.

GLOSSARY

aquatic: of or relating to water; living or growing in water.

breed (v): to mate a male and a female for the purpose of producing young.

carcass: the dead body of an animal.

colonize: to set up a group or community where all members work or live together.

common: occurring or appearing frequently.

court: to try gaining favor from another with attention and gifts. Many animals court one another when choosing mates.

crest: a growth, such as a tuft of feathers, on top of an animal's head.

cultivate: to improve and prepare land, by plowing and fertilizing, for raising crops.

current: a flowing mass of air or water.

equator: an imaginary line around Earth that lies halfway between the North and South poles. The equator divides Earth into the Northern Hemisphere and the Southern Hemisphere. The climate at the equator is hot and humid.

estival: of or relating to summer. Estival birds remain in the same place only for the summer season. They migrate during winter to a warmer climate.

evolution: the process of changing or developing gradually from one form to another. Over time, all living things must evolve to survive in their changing environments, or they may become extinct.

fledgling: a young bird that is learning to fly. Some fledglings migrate with adult birds.

flight: a group, especially of birds or aircraft, flying together.

flock: a group of animals, such as some types of birds, that live, travel, or find food together.

glide: to move slowly, quietly, and easily from one place to another without adding power to the wing movement.

gonads: organs that produce the reproductive cells of a body; ovaries produce ova, and testicles produce sperm.

habitat: the natural home of a plant or animal.

hormones: substances produced by glands in the body and carried through the blood to different organs and tissues. Hormones regulate some bodily functions and control growth.

incubate: to keep eggs warm, usually with body heat, so they will hatch.

lagoon: a shallow lake that opens into a sea or a river.

locust: a type of grasshopper that often travels in swarms and causes damage to vegetation.

majestic: grand; stately.

marsh: waterlogged ground; swampy land.

mate (v): to join together (animals) to produce young.

migrate: to move from one place or climate to another, usually on a seasonal basis.

moss: small, dense, green plants that do not produce flowers and that grow on tree trunks, rock, and damp ground.

nest (v): to build a snug, cozy shelter and live there.

ornithologists: scientists who study birds.

overcast: clouded over; obscured with clouds or mist; gloomy.

plumage: the feathers of a bird.

polar: relating to those regions of Earth that are very cold and icy. The climate of polar regions, such as the North Pole and the South Pole, is harsh to humans, but many animals can live in these areas.

predators: animals that kill and eat other animals.

prey: animals that are hunted, captured, and killed for food by other animals.

quill: the larger feathers of the wings or tail of a bird.

remote: far away; distant.

retina: a lining on the inside of the

eyeball that is sensitive to light. The retina receives the visual image that enters the eye through the lens and sends it along the optic nerve to the brain.

sedentary: remaining in one area; not migrating.

species: animals or plants that are closely related and often similar in behavior and appearance. Members of the same species are able to breed together.

subcutaneous: located or found just beneath the skin.

tropics: the region centered on the equator and lying between the Tropic of Cancer (23.5 degrees north of the equator) and the Tropic of Capricorn (23.5 degrees south of the equator.) This region is typically very hot and humid.

vertebrates: animals that have backbones, such as fish, frogs, reptiles, mammals, and birds.

ACTIVITIES

◆ Visit a bird display in a natural history museum, or find a book with lots of good pictures of birds. Examine the size and shape of the beak that different kinds of birds have. Sketch as many different beaks as you can find. Next to each sketch write the kind of bird that has the beak, what it eats, and how it gets its food. How does the shape of a bird's beak help it feed? Do different birds living in the same habitat have similar beaks? Can you explain your answer?

◆ Visit a zoo that has storks. Observe the different kinds of storks the zoo houses. How are they the same? In what ways are they different? Are there other kinds of birds with similar features, such as long legs and long necks? Compare these birds with the storks. Where do these other birds live in the wild? Do they eat the same kinds of food as the storks do? Do they migrate? If so, how far do they fly, and where do they go? Draw some of the bird migration paths on a map so you can compare distances and routes.

MORE BOOKS TO READ

Big Birds. Denise Casey (Dutton)
The Bird Atlas. Richard Orr (Dorling Kindersley)
Birds, Birds, Birds. National Wildlife Federation Staff (National Wildlife)
Birds Do the Strangest Things. A. and L. Hornblow (Random House)
Birds and How They Live. (Dorling Kindersley)
Crinkleroot's Guide to Knowing the Birds. Jim Arnosky (Macmillan)
Extremely Weird Birds. Sarah Lovett (John Muir)
Miserable Marabou. Franz Berliner (Gareth Stevens)
A Picture Book of Water Birds. Grace Mabie (Troll Associates)
Stewart Stork. Ross M. Madsen (Dial Books)
Waterfowl. Dave Beaty (Child's World)

VIDEOS

Big Birds. Animal Profile series. (Rainbow Educational Video)
Birds. All About Animals series. (AIMS Media.)
Birds and Migration. (International Film Bureau)
Flight for Survival: The Migration of Birds. (Encyclopædia Britannica
    Educational Corporation)

PLACES TO VISIT

St. Louis Zoological Park
Forest Park
St. Louis, MO 63110

Henry Doorly Zoo
3701 South 10th Street
Omaha, NE 68107

Stanley Park Zoo
Stanley Park
Vancouver, British
    Columbia V6B 3X8

Metropolitan Toronto Zoo
Meadowvale Road
West Hill
Toronto, Ontario
M1E 4R5

**Royal Melbourne
    Zoological Gardens**
Elliott Avenue
Parkville, Victoria
Australia 3052

Taronga Zoo
Bradleys Head Road
Mosman, New South Wales
Australia 2088

Auckland Zoological Park
Motions Road
Western Springs
Auckland 2
New Zealand

INDEX

Answers to BIRD SECRETS questions:
1. c
2. a
3. b
4. a
5. b
6. b